Date: 8/30/21

J 954.96 GLA
Glaser, Chaya,
Nepal /

PALM BEACH COUNTY
LIBRARY SYSTEM
3650 SUMMIT BLVD.
WEST PALM BEACH, FL 33406

Countries We Come From

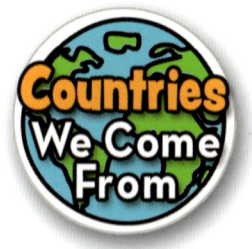

Nepal

by Chaya Glaser

Consultant: Marjorie Faulstich Orellana, PhD
Professor of Urban Schooling
University of California, Los Angeles

BEARPORT PUBLISHING
New York, New York

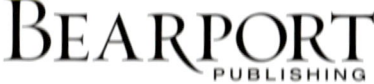

Credits

Cover, © Rido/Shutterstock and © Daniel Prudek/iStock; TOC, © Daniel Prudek/Shutterstock; 4, © MarBom/Shutterstock; 5T, © Hadynyah/iStock; 5B, © Daniel Prudek/iStock; 7, © fotoVoyager/iStock; 8T, © Quick Shot/Shutterstock; 8B, © Shree Krishna Photo/Shutterstock; 9, © LeoPatrizi/iStock; 10–11, © Vixit/Shutterstock; 11B, © Westend61 GmbH/Alamy; 12, © Zzvet/Shutterstock; 13, © fotoVoyager/iStock; 14, © FLPA/Alamy; 15T, © Sainam51/Shutterstock; 15B, © ewastudio/iStock; 16R, © Alexandra Lande/Shutterstock; 16B, © Gopal Chitrakar/Reuters/Newscom; 17, © Fotos593/Shutterstock; 18, © Bartosz Hadyniak/iStock; 19, © dbimages/Alamy; 20L, © Sunny Shrestha/iStock; 20–21, © Stephanie Bidouze/Shutterstock; 22, © Eye Ubiquitous/AGE Fotostock; 23, © Pascal Mannaerts/Alamy; 24, © CRS Photo/Shutterstock; 25T, © Design Pics Inc/Alamy; 25B, © Sunil Pradhan/NurPhoto/Sipa USA/Newscom; 26, © 4kodiak/iStock; 27, © Xinhua/Alamy; 28, © SoumenNath/iStock; 29, © Dutourdumonde Photography/Shutterstock; 30T, © Charles O. Cecil/Alamy and © Wrangel/Dreamstime; 30B, © Christophe Cappelli/Shutterstock; 31 (T to B), © Jakub Cejpek/Shutterstock, © ONGshutterstock/Shutterstock, © Nowamhere/Shutterstock, © vectorx2263/Shutterstock, © Daniel Prudek/Shutterstock, and © Caroline Lib33/Shutterstock; 32, © tristan tan/Shutterstock.

Publisher: Kenn Goin
Senior Editor: Joyce Tavolacci
Creative Director: Spencer Brinker
Design: Debrah Kaiser
Photo Researcher: Thomas Persano

Library of Congress Cataloging-in-Publication Data

Names: Glaser, Chaya, author.
Title: Nepal / by Chaya Glaser.
Description: New York, New York : Bearport Publishing, [2019] | Series: Countries we come from | Includes bibliographical references and index.
Identifiers: LCCN 2018044159 (print) | LCCN 2018044964 (ebook) | ISBN 9781642802665 (ebook) | ISBN 9781642801972 (library bound)
Subjects: LCSH: Nepal—Juvenile literature.
Classification: LCC DS493.4 (ebook) | LCC DS493.4 .G55 2019 (print) | DDC 954.96—dc23
LC record available at https://lccn.loc.gov/2018044159

Copyright © 2019 Bearport Publishing Company, Inc. All rights reserved. No part of this publication may be reproduced in whole or in part, stored in any retrieval system, or transmitted in any form or by any means, electronic, mechanical, photocopying, recording, or otherwise, without written permission from the publisher.

For more information, write to Bearport Publishing Company, Inc., 45 West 21st Street, Suite 3B, New York, New York 10010. Printed in the United States of America.

10 9 8 7 6 5 4 3 2 1

Contents

This Is Nepal............. 4

Fast Facts................30

Glossary 31

Index 32

Read More 32

Learn More Online 32

About the Author 32

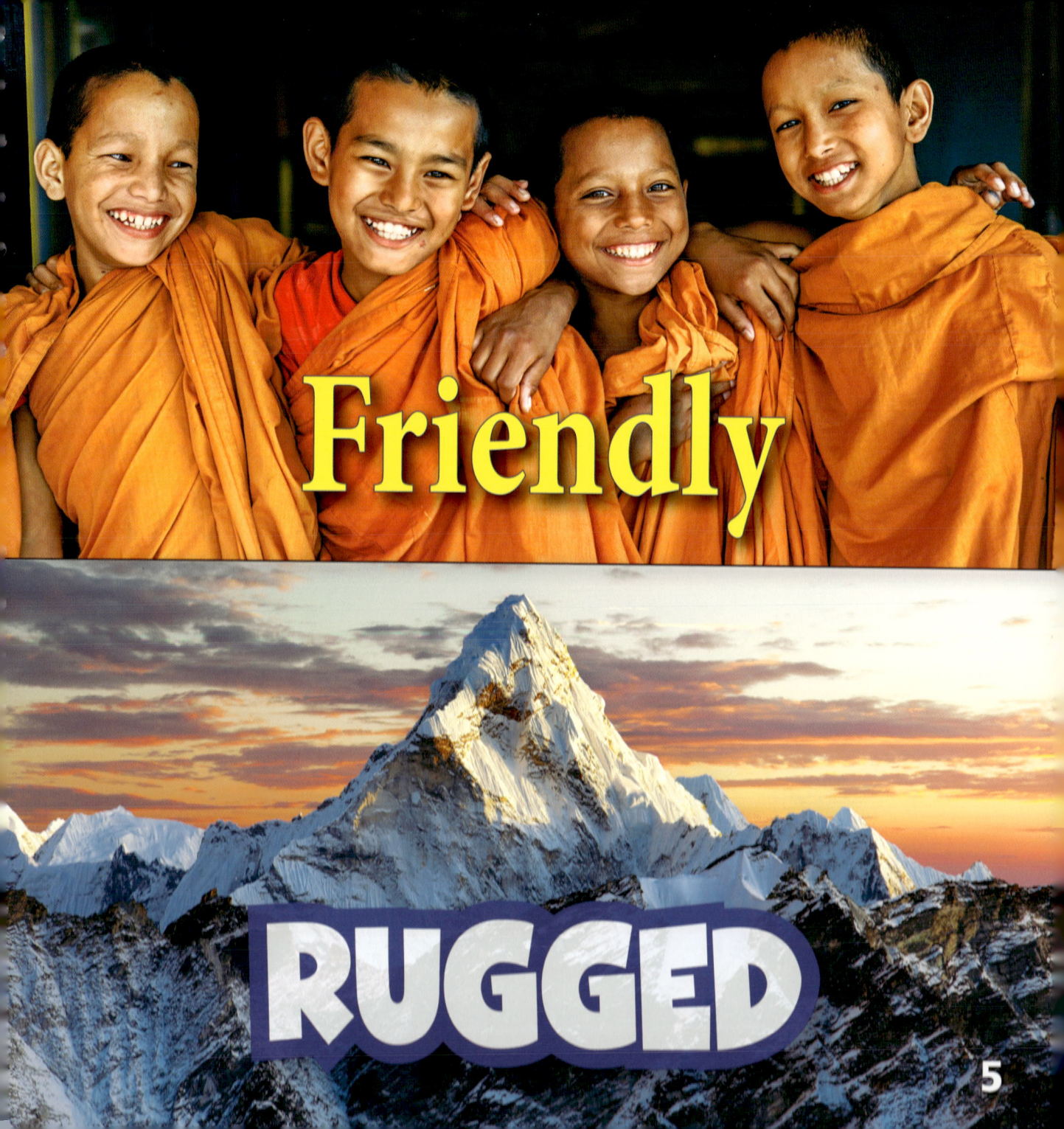
Friendly

RUGGED

Nepal is a small country in South Asia.

It's about the same size as the state of Arkansas.

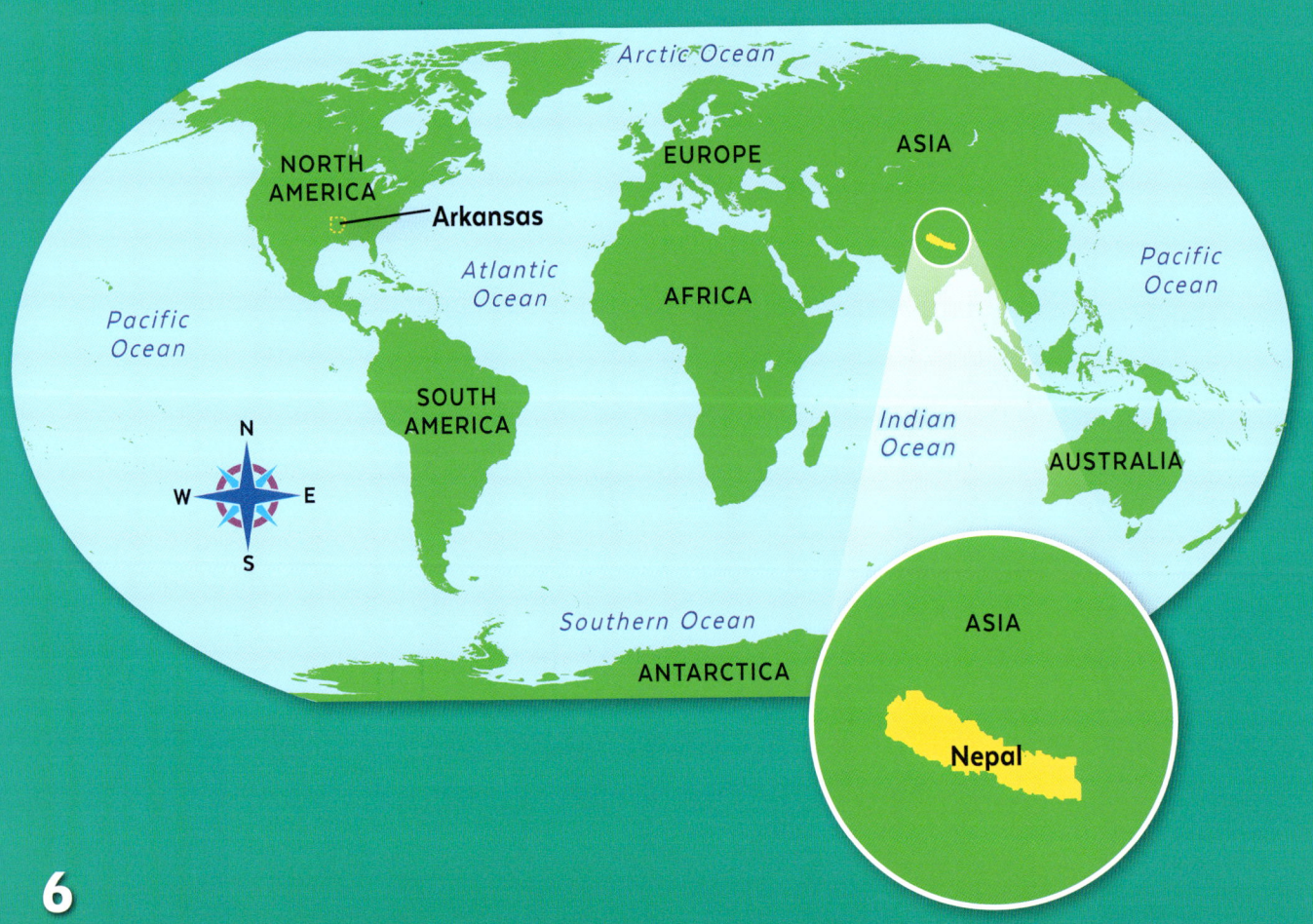

Over 29 million people live in Nepal.

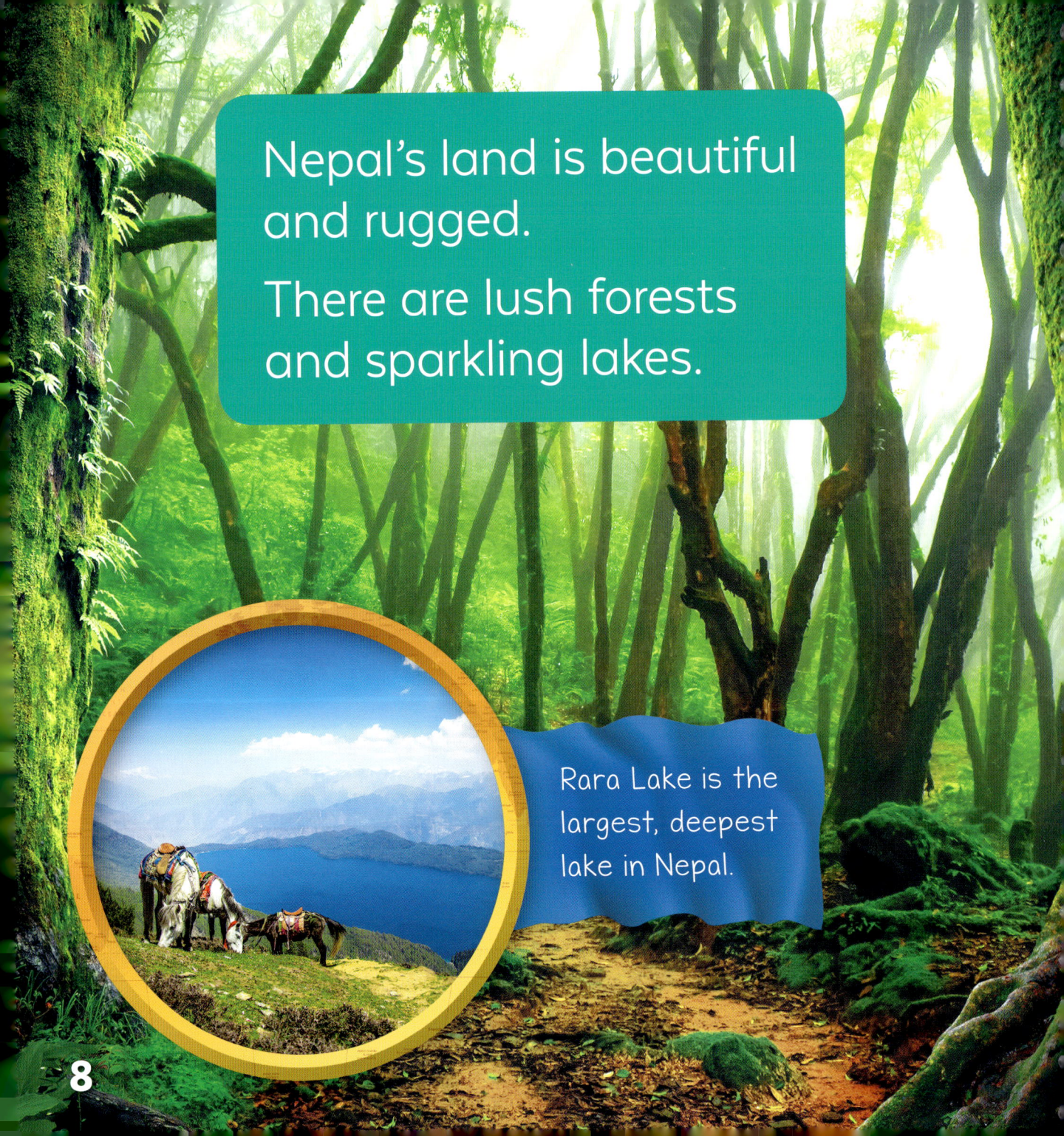

Nepal's land is beautiful and rugged.

There are lush forests and sparkling lakes.

Rara Lake is the largest, deepest lake in Nepal.

Snowy mountains cover much of the country.

In fact, the world's tallest mountains are in Nepal!

Mount Everest towers above the clouds.

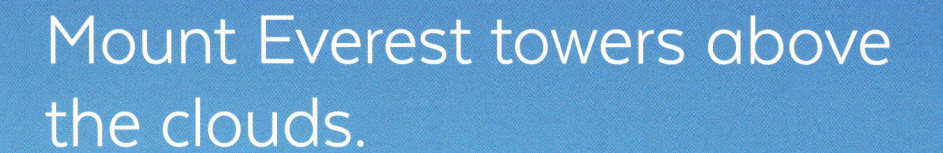

It's the highest mountain on Earth!

People come from all over the world to climb it.

Mt. Everest is 29,029 feet (8,848 m) tall!

Mount Everest is part of a mountain range called the Himalayas.

Only a few people reach the top.

Sherpas are people who live high in the mountains.

They are expert climbers.

They often guide people up the steep **peaks**.

Some Sherpas raise yaks. Yaks help carry heavy bags up and down the mountains.

13

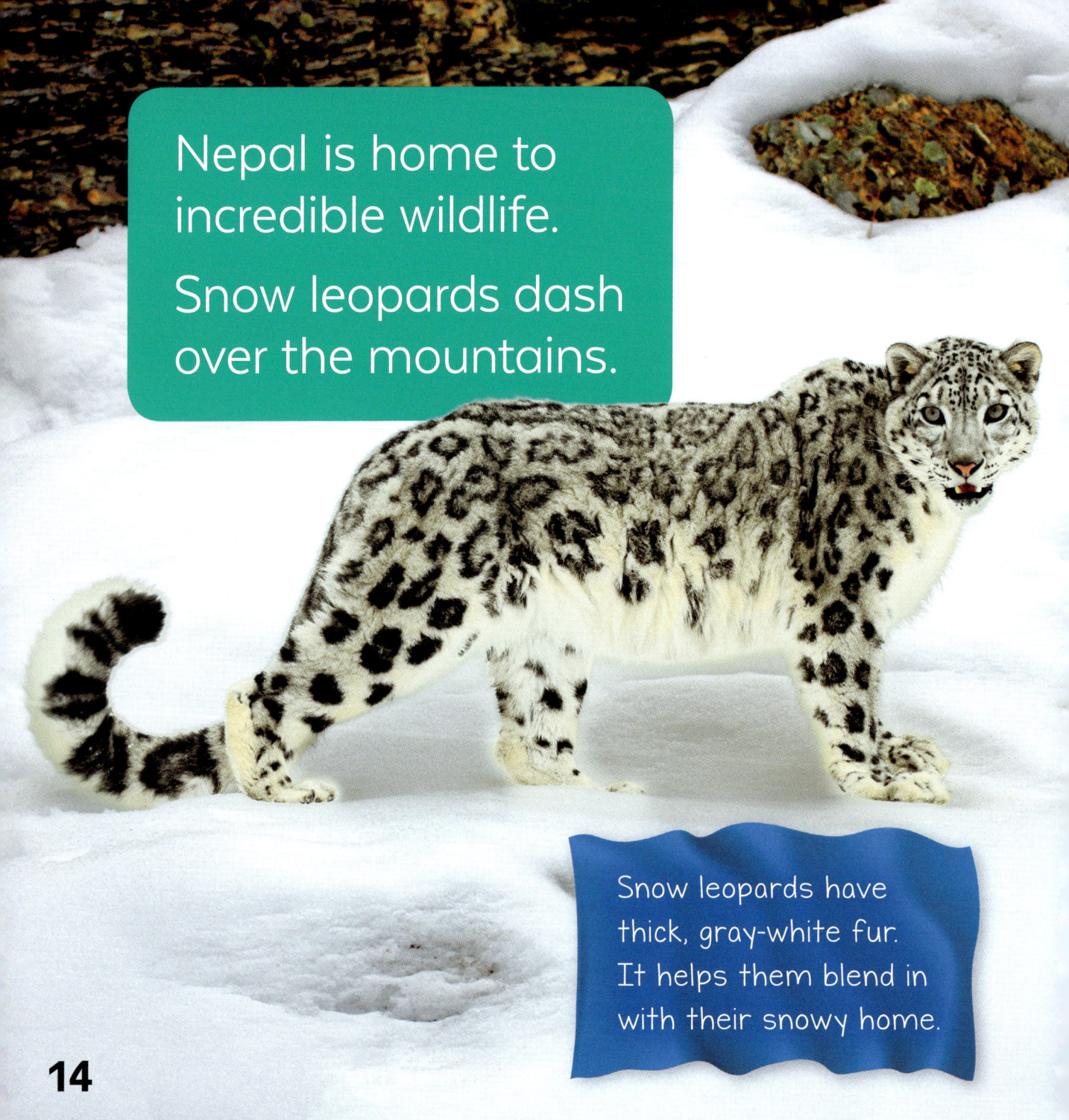

Nepal is home to incredible wildlife.

Snow leopards dash over the mountains.

Snow leopards have thick, gray-white fur. It helps them blend in with their snowy home.

Huge vultures circle the skies.

Bengal tigers crawl through thick forests.

For hundreds of years, kings ruled Nepal.

The Nepali people wanted more freedom.

a royal palace

Finally, in 2008, the king stepped down.

King Gyanendra, Nepal's last king

16

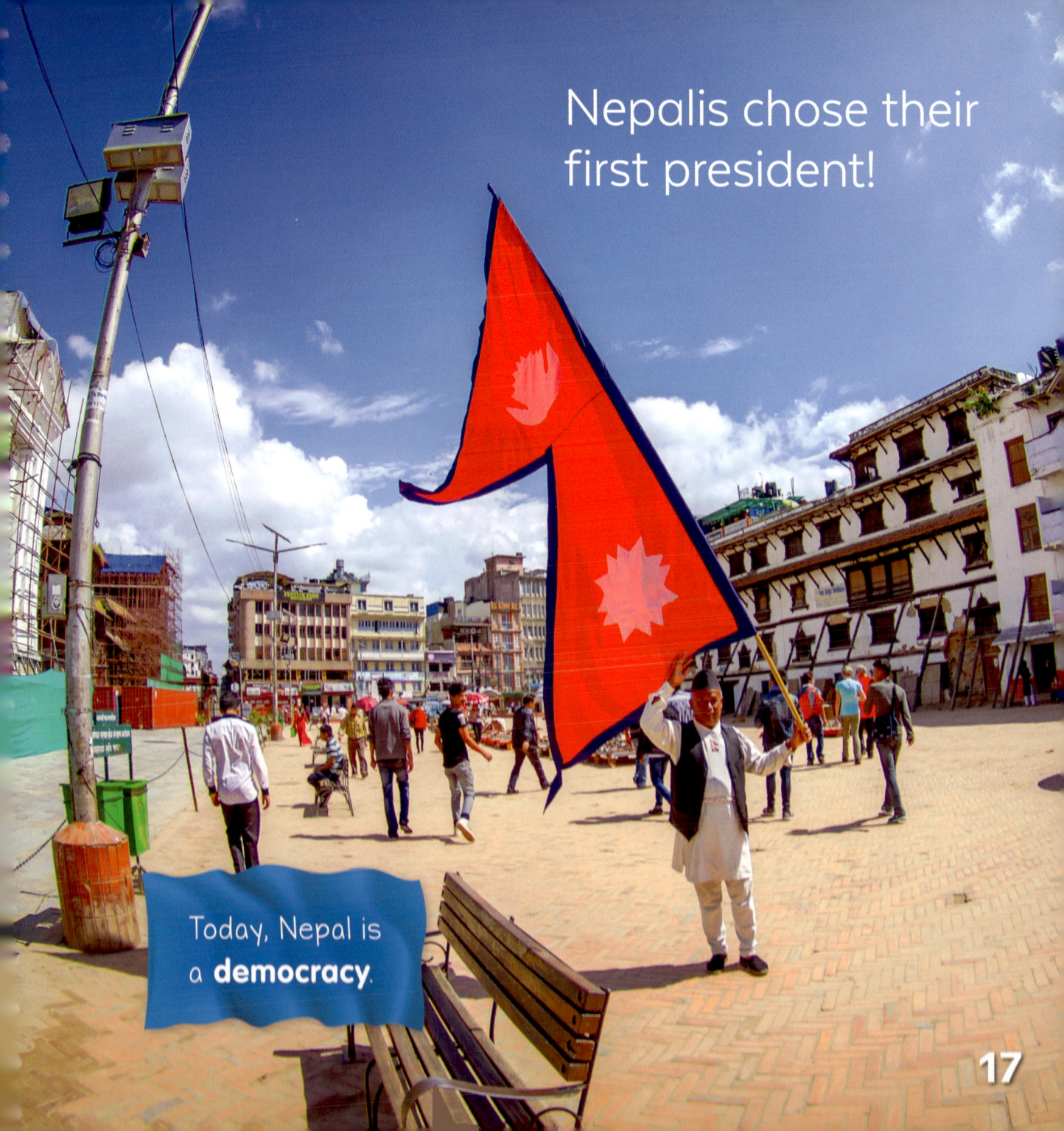

Nepalis chose their first president!

Today, Nepal is a **democracy**.

Religion is important to Nepali people. Most people are Hindu or Buddhist. They worship in colorful **temples**.

Hindu holy men

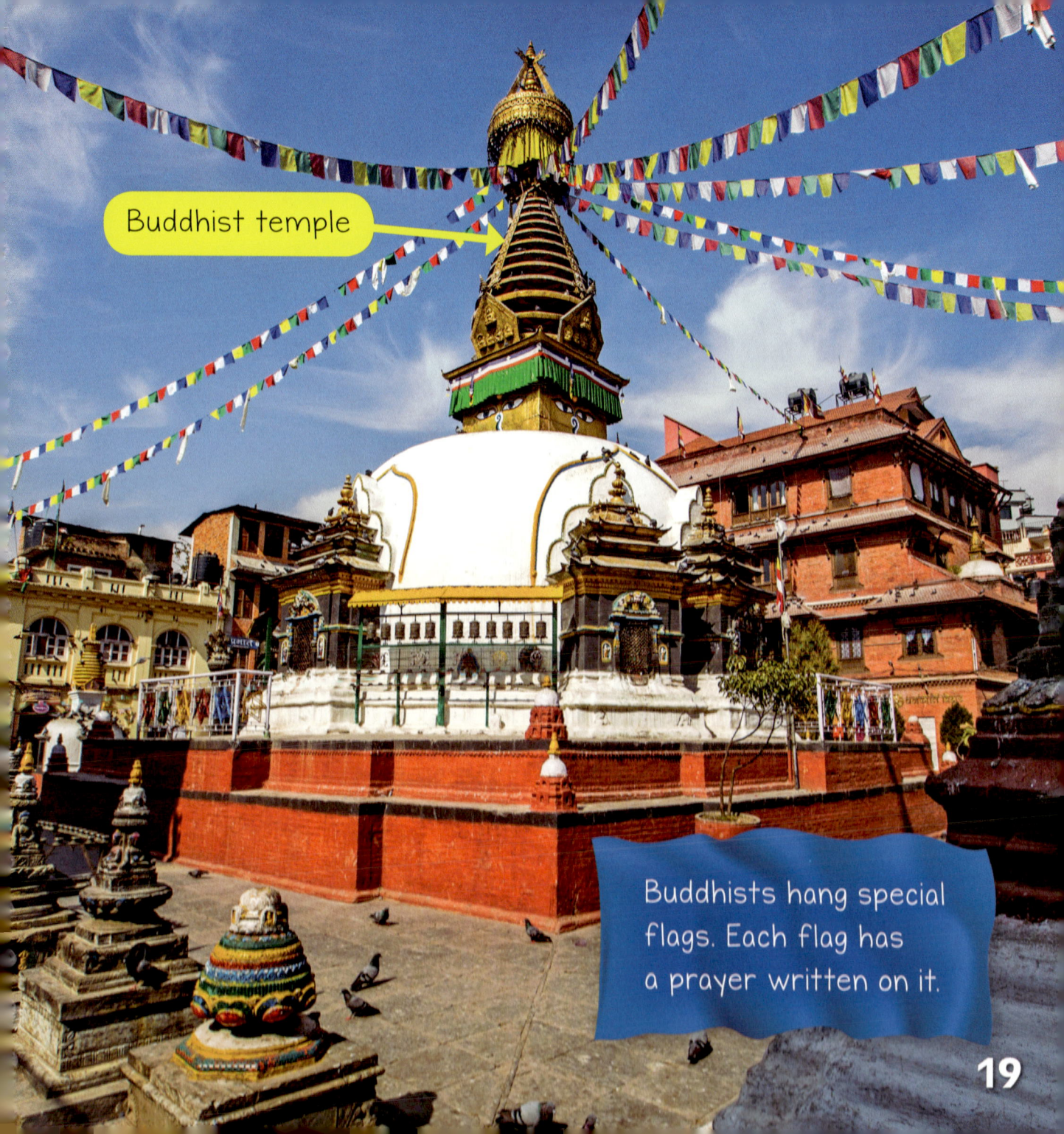

Buddhist temple

Buddhists hang special flags. Each flag has a prayer written on it.

Kathmandu (kat-man-DOO) is Nepal's largest city.

It's also the **capital**.

The city has many lively markets and temples.

One famous temple is home to monkeys!

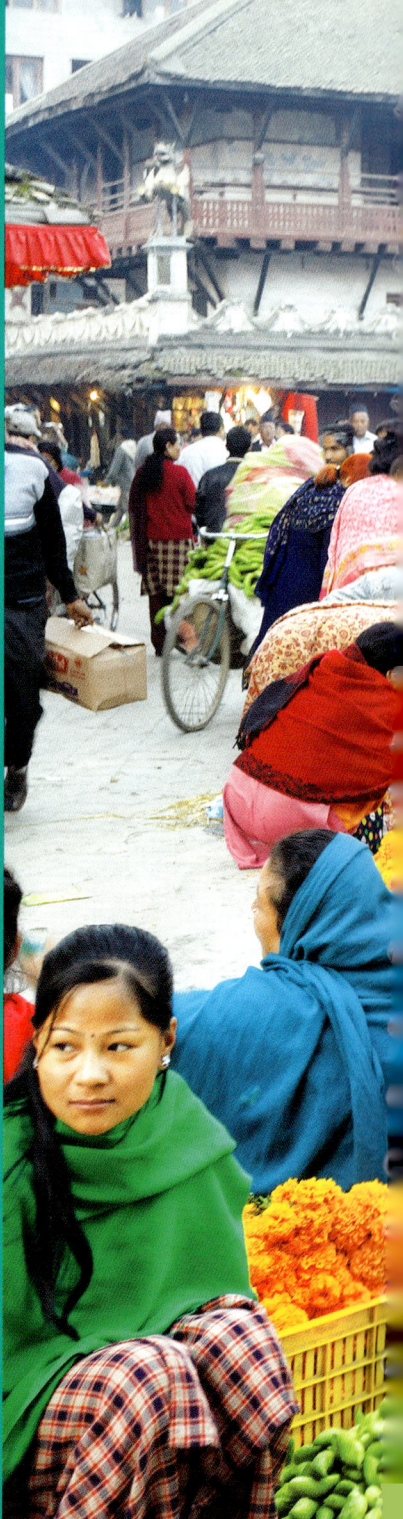

Morning Market in Kathmandu

The main language in Nepal is Nepali.

Hello and *goodbye* are the same word in Nepali:

Namaste
(nah-muh-STAY)

This is how you say *friend*:

Mitra
(MEE-truh)

Over 90 different languages are spoken in Nepal!

A ball flies over a net. Volleyball is Nepal's national sport.

People also love playing soccer.

Nepalis enjoy riding horses, too.

It's time to eat!

Nepali people like *momos*.

Momos are dumplings filled with vegetables or meat.

In Nepal, most people only eat with their right hand.

People also enjoy *dal bhat*, a hearty lentil stew.

Every year, people celebrate *Tihar*. It's a **festival** of light and life. Nepalis light lamps.

People also **honor** their pet dogs!

Tihar lasts for five days. Day two is Dog Tihar. Nepalis put flowers on their pets!

Fast Facts

Capital city: Kathmandu

Population of Nepal: Over 29 million

Main language: Nepali

Money: Nepalese rupee

Major religions: Hinduism and Buddhism

Neighboring countries include: India and the land of Tibet

Cool Fact: Nepal's flag is made of two triangles. The shapes represent the Himalayan Mountains!

Glossary

capital (KAP-uh-tuhl) the city where a country's government is based

democracy (dih-MOK-ruh-see) a system of government in which people choose their leaders

festival (FES-tuh-vuhl) a celebration

honor (ON-ur) to show great respect

peaks (PEEKS) the pointed tops of mountains

temples (TEM-puhlz) buildings where people go to pray and worship

Index

animals 13, 14–15
capital 20–21, 30
cities 20–21, 30
festivals 28–29
food 26–27
history 16–17
language 22–23, 30
mountains 10–11, 12–13, 14, 30
nature 8–9, 10–11
religion 18–19
Sherpas 12–13
sports 24–25

Read More

Adhikary, Anita. *N is for Nepal.* Herndon, VA: Mascot Books (2011).

Owings, Lisa. *Nepal (Exploring Countries).* Minnetonka, MN: Bellwether (2014).

Learn More Online

To learn more about Nepal, visit
www.bearportpublishing.com/CountriesWeComeFrom

About the Author

Chaya Glaser loves traveling and learning about colorful cultures around the world. She especially enjoys finding new places to hike.